INTRODUCTION

You bought a guitar...so now what?

Congratulations! You look great holding that new guitar (even standing in front of the mirror, lip-synching to the radio, swinging your hips back and forth). But won't your friends and family be even more impressed if you can actually play the darn thing? In just a couple of weeks, we'll have you playing some very well-known tunes, as well as jamming on some new ones. By the end of this book, it's on to the hits—The Beatles, Clapton, Hendrix and many more.

All we ask is that you observe the three Ps: **patience**, **practice** and **pace yourself**.

Don't try to bite off more than you can chew, and DON'T skip ahead. If your fingers hurt, take the day off. If you get frustrated, put it down and come back later. If you forget something, go back and learn it again. If you're having a great time, forget about dinner and keep on playing. Most importantly, have fun!

ABOUT THE CD

(...no, it's not a coaster!)

Glad you noticed the added bonus—a CD! Each music example in the book is included on the CD, so you can hear how it sounds and play along when you're ready. Take a listen whenever you see this symbol: **◆1**

Each example on the CD is preceded by one measure of "clicks" to indicate the tempo and meter. Also, a variety of guitars and grooves are used.

Pan right to hear the guitar part emphasized. Pan left to hear the accompaniment emphasized. As you become more confident, try playing the guitar part along with the rest of the band (the accompaniment).

7777 W. BLUEMOUND RD. P.O. BOX 13819 MILWAUKEE, WI 53213

Copyright © 1997 by HAL LEONARD CORPORATION
International Copyright Secured   All Rights Reserved

Visit Hal Leonard on the internet at http: // www.halleonard.com

A GOOD PLACE TO START

Your guitar is your friend...

A guitar can be like a good friend over the years—get you through the rough times and help you sing away the blues. In fact, many famous players give their favorite six-stringed friend a name. Willie Nelson calls his guitar "Trigger." B.B. King calls his "Lucille." Eric Clapton calls his "Blackie."

What a beauty!

Below are pictures of a standard electric guitar and a standard acoustic (steel-string) guitar. Get acquainted with the parts of your guitar, and don't forget to give it a name.

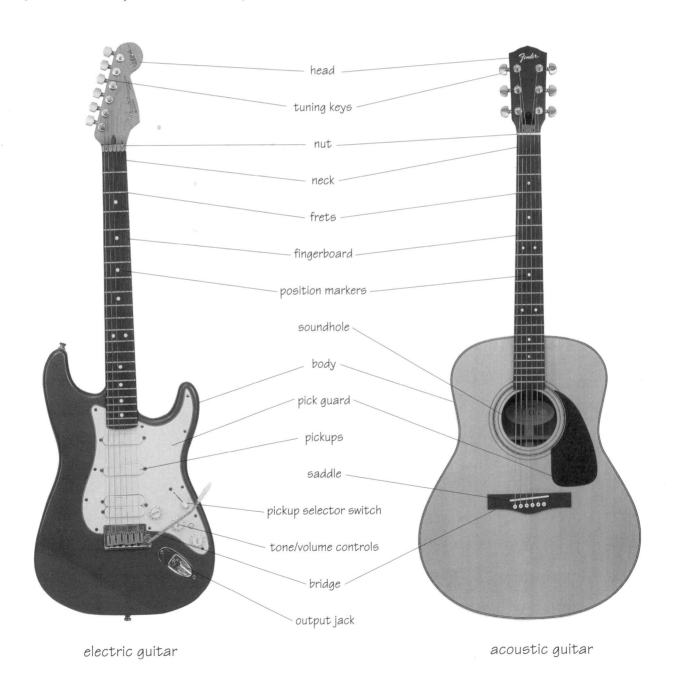

head

tuning keys

nut

neck

frets

fingerboard

position markers

soundhole

body

pick guard

pickups

saddle

pickup selector switch

tone/volume controls

bridge

output jack

electric guitar

acoustic guitar

TUNING

When you tune, you correct the pitch of each string. **Pitch** means how high or low a musical tone is. This is adjusted by tightening (or loosening) the string, using the tuning keys on the head of the guitar. The tighter the string, the higher the pitch.

Your six guitar strings should be tuned to the pitches **E-B-G-D-A-E**.

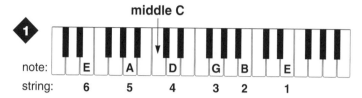

CAUTION: Tighten slowly and not too much, or you'll be heading back to the store to buy new strings!

Piano tuning

No, you aren't about to tune an entire piano! If you have a piano or electric keyboard nearby, play the above notes one at a time and tune the corresponding guitar string until its pitch matches that of the piano.

Electric tuner

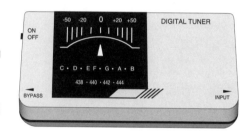

If you don't have the luxury of a piano or keyboard, you may want to purchase an electric guitar tuner.

A tuner will "listen" to each string as you play it and indicate whether the pitch is too high or too low.

Don't give up hope...if you don't have a piano and you can't buy a tuner, there's yet another solution:

Relative tuning

To tune your guitar by ear, you must tune the strings to each other. This is done in the following manner:

 Assuming string 6 is tuned correctly to E, press string 6 behind fret 5, play the depressed string 6 and open string 5 together. When the two sounds match, you're in tune.

 Press string 5 behind fret 5 and tune open string 4 to it.

 Press string 4 behind fret 5 and tune open string 3 to it.

 Press string 3 behind fret 4 and tune open string 2 to it.

 Press the string 2 behind fret 5 and tune string 1 to it.

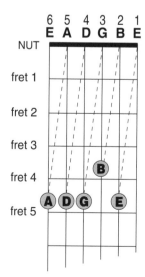

A FEW MORE THINGS

...before we jam!

Sit down and stay a while...

Perhaps the most comfortable and least tiring way to learn guitar is to sit while playing.

Once you learn a few tunes, feel free to stand up, lay down, hold it behind your head, or whatever. But for now let's put that extra effort to better use—playing.

sitting

standing

Please hold...

Hold the neck of the guitar with your **left hand**, with the thumb resting comfortably behind the neck.

Hold the neck of the guitar slightly upwards—not downwards (at least not until you're on stage in front of thousands of fans and you're screaming through a solo).

Hold the pick in your **right hand** (when you're more advanced you can use your teeth, Jimi Hendrix-style).

left hand position (fingers)

left hand position (thumb)

right hand (with pick)

There's nothing stressful here, so don't grip the neck of your guitar too hard (you might strangle it!)

Picture This...

Fingerboard diagrams (or "grids") picture a portion of the fretboard and show you where to play the notes and chords. Circles with note names are drawn onto the diagram to indicate the notes played.

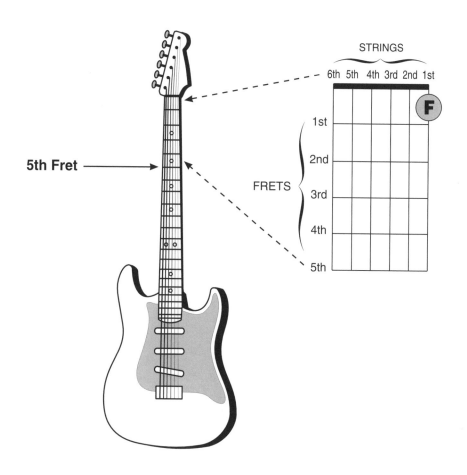

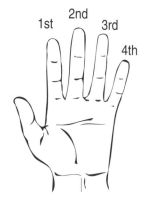

Think of your left-hand fingers as being numbered 1 through 4.

DOG-EAR THESE TWO PAGES
(...you'll need to review them later)

...anguage with its own symbols, structure, rules (and exceptions to those rules). ...e, and play music requires knowing all the symbols and rules. But let's take it one step at a time (a few now, a few later)...

Notes

Music is written with little doo-hickeys called **notes.** Notes come in all shapes and sizes. A note has two essential characteristics: its **pitch** (indicated by its position on the staff) and its **rhythmic value** (indicated by the following symbols):

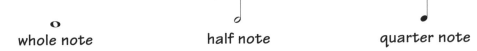

The rhythmic value lets you know how many beats the note lasts. Most commonly, a quarter note equals one beat. After that it's just like fractions (we hate math, too!):

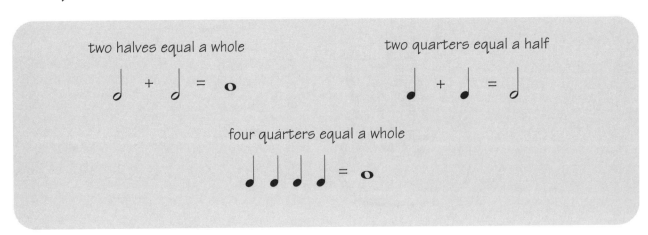

Staff

All the notes are positioned on (or nearby) a **staff**, which consists of five parallel lines and four spaces. (The plural for staff is "staves.") Each line and space represents a different pitch.

Leger Lines

Since not all notes will fit on just five lines and four spaces, **leger lines** (pronounced like "ledger") are used to extend the staff:

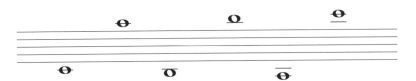

Clef

A symbol called a **clef** indicates which pitches appear on a particular staff. Music uses a variety of clefs, but we are only concerned with one for now:

Treble clef

A **treble clef** staff makes the lines and spaces have the following pitches:

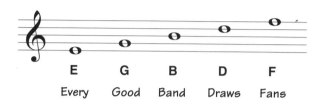

E	G	B	D	F
Every	Good	Band	Draws	Fans

F A C E

"FACE"

An easy way to remember the line pitches is "**E**very **G**ood **B**and **D**raws **F**ans." For the spaces, spell "**face**."

Measures (or Bars)

Notes on a staff are divided into **measures** (or "bars") to help you keep track of where you are in the song. (Imagine reading a book without any periods, commas, or capital letters!)

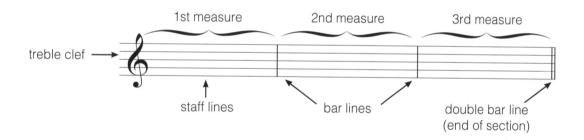

Time Signatures (or Meters)

A **time signature** (or "meter") indicates how many beats will appear in each measure. It contains two numbers: the top number tells you how many beats will be in each measure; the bottom number says what type of note will equal one beat.

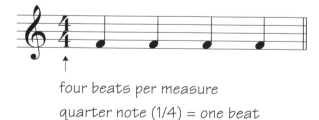

four beats per measure
quarter note (1/4) = one beat

three beats per measure
quarter note (1/4) = one beat

> **R**elax for a while, read through it again later, and then move on.
> (Trust us — as we go through the book, you'll start to understand it.)

LESSON 1
Don't just sit there, play something!

We're tuned. We're relaxed. We're comfortable. And we're eager to play. Let's get down to business...

As you know from page 4, the left hand "selects" a note by depressing a string at a fret, while the right hand "plays" that string with the pick. Playing an **open string** means playing a string without pressing a fret.

String 1: E

Forget 2-6, let's concentrate on string 1 for now. Use the photos and fingerboard diagrams to play your first notes.

 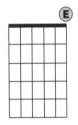   Play string 1 open and you will hear E. This note is indicated on a treble clef staff like this:

 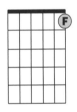   Play string 1 while pressing fret 1 with finger 1 and you will hear F. This note is indicated on the staff like this:

    Press fret 3 with finger 3 and play G. (You can leave finger 1 on fret 1, if you like.) You guessed it, the note on the staff looks like this: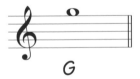

> **"What happened to fret 2?"**
> That note is F-sharp. We'll explain "sharps" later.

Put it to good use...

Three notes in about three minutes—not bad progress, huh? Practice these notes again and again using the following tunes. (If you need a review of rhythmic values or time signatures, turn back to pages 6 and 7.)

② E–F–G

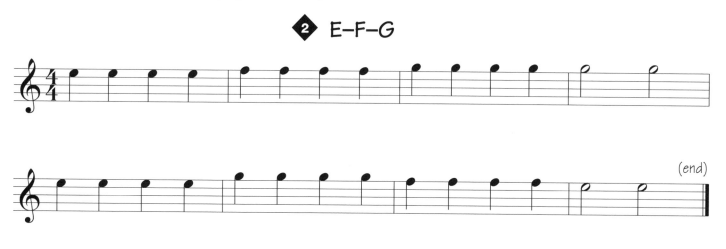

(end)

Just like reading a book, go to the next line in the song as soon as you reach the end of each staff. However, when you see this symbol (▤▏), you are at the end of that song.

③ First Song

☞ **Fingering Tip #1:** When pressing a fret, use only the fingertip (not the whole finger, silly!), so that other strings are not touched by the same finger.

④ Three-Note Rock

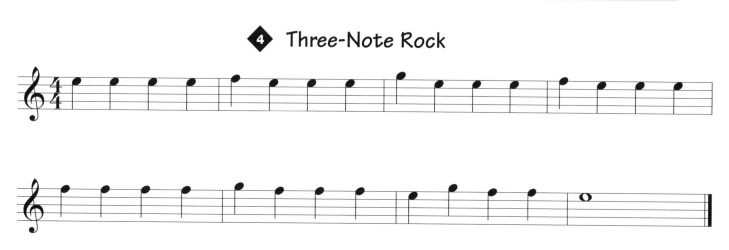

Don't be afraid to repeat these tunes over and over, playing them a little bit faster each time. Then, when you're ready (and after a snack from the 'fridge), we'll move on to Lesson 2.

LESSON 2
Moving on...

Welcome back! Now you know three notes and three songs. Okay, we admit they were boring ones, but let's learn three more notes and some better songs.

HELPFUL HINT: Take a few seconds, flip back to page 3 and make sure your guitar is still in tune. (If the cat starts screaming, it probably isn't!)

String 2: B

We'll learn string 2 the same way we learned string 1 (yes, even skipping poor ol' fret 2 again). The only difference is the new pitches you will hear:

 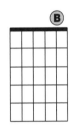
Play string 2 open. That's B. This note lies on the middle line of the treble clef staff:
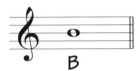
B

Play string 2 while pressing fret 1 with finger 1 and you get C, which lies on the space just above B:

C

 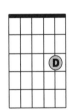
Press fret 3 with finger 3 and you have D. It sits just above C:
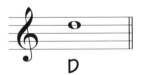
D

👉 **W**hy not fret 2 again? This time fret 2 is C-sharp.
But since you keep asking, we'll introduce "sharps" in Lesson 3.

Put it to more good use...

Practice your new notes with this short exercise:

5 B–C–D

Now here are some tunes (much better ones, we might add) to practice your six notes. Don't be embarassed to review E, F, and G again before playing.

6 Ode to Joyful Rock

☞ **Fingering Tip #2:** When changing fingers from string 1 to string 2, try to let your eyes move ahead in the music and move the correct finger to the correct string before the next note occurs.

7 Blues for My Dog

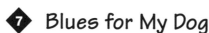

Remember to keep your fingers arched at all times (while playing, that is).

8 Rock to My Lou

9 Rockin' the Bells

☞ **Fingering Tip #3:** When playing a higher note, leave the lower note depressed. For example, leave finger 1 on F while pressing finger 3 on G. When you go back to F, simply lift finger 3.

10 Give My Regards to Broadway

If your fingertips hurt, take a break. But never fear—the more you practice, the faster they will toughen up. (Hey, no pain...no gain!)

SOME MORE NOTES ON MUSIC
(...pardon the pun!)

Before we go to Lesson 3, we want to tell you some more about the hieroglyphics of music.

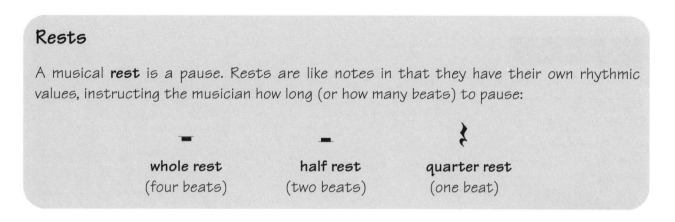

Rests

A musical **rest** is a pause. Rests are like notes in that they have their own rhythmic values, instructing the musician how long (or how many beats) to pause:

whole rest
(four beats)

half rest
(two beats)

quarter rest
(one beat)

In the following 4/4 example, you will play E, E, pause, E, pause, pause, pause, pause, E, E, pause, pause, E, pause, pause, E:

♦11 Take a Load Off

IMPORTANT: A rest does not mean rest your fingers or put down your guitar! During a rest, you should get your fingers into position for the next set of notes.

♦12 When the Saints Go Marching In

LESSON 3
Three's company...

Unbelievable—six notes already. You're a fast learner! How 'bout another string? (Make sure you're still in tune, if not—page 3.)

String 3: G

String 3 is a bit different from strings 1 and 2. (Sure, it's thicker!) String 3 will get finger 2 into the action, and we'll skip fret 1 this time...

 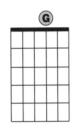

Play string 3 open. That's G, which is written on the second line of the treble clef staff:

 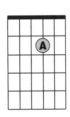

Play string 3 while pressing fret 2 with finger 2 and you get A. This note lies on the space between G and B:

☞ We realize that you already learned another G on string 1, but since the musical alphabet only has the letters A through G, this type of repetition will eventually occur with all note names.

Let's practice these two new notes. (WARNING: With only two notes, this exercise is rather boring. Hang in there...)

⑬ Two-Note Jam

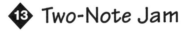

Only after you're convinced you know these two notes, should you move on to the next page...

14 Yankee Doodle

Remember to practice slowly. Speed up the **tempo** as you become more confident with the notes.

15 Red River Rock

If you need, put the guitar down and just recite the note names of the song. Then practice locating the notes on the guitar before actually playing. Most importantly, just have fun!

16 Aura Lee

Take a break, get some sleep, maybe some breakfast.
When you return, review Lessons 1, 2, and 3.

YOU LOOK SHARP!

Music is made up of **half steps** and **whole steps**. Each fret on your guitar equals one half step. When a song requires a note to be only a half step higher or lower, a symbol is placed by that note.

One half step higher is called a **sharp** and looks like a tic-tac-toe board: ♯

One half-step lower is called a **flat** and looks like a backwards note with no air in it: ♭

EXCEPTION TO THE RULE: From E to F is only a half step; from B to C is only a half step. (Look at the white keys on the piano diagram on page 3.)

Since you only got two notes in Lesson 3...

We'll give you not one but two more notes! And they're both sharps!! Return to strings 1 and 2 and check 'em out.

  On string 1, press fret 2 with finger 2 and hear your first sharp:

 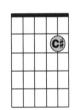 On string 2, press fret 2 with finger 2 and you'll hear C-sharp: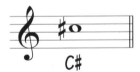

Try this short exercise with your new "sharp-looking" (couldn't resist) notes:

⟨17⟩ I Know Two Sharps

Now you know why we skipped fret 2 earlier...
On string 1 (E), one fret higher than F is F-sharp.
On string 2 (B), one fret higher than C is C-sharp.

18 Rockin' Sharps

Good Groove! Please, practice patiently prior to proceeding. (Say it fast five times! Play it fast five times!)

19 This Old Man

☞ A **natural** sign (♮) cancels an accidental on a note, returning it to its natural pitch.

20 Private Eye Groove

☞ Hey, look over here! Watch the music, not your fingers!
(Your brain has enough going on—don't try to memorize the tunes, too!)

LESSON 4

A little bit lower now...

Let's check your progress: three strings and ten notes. It's like eating chips—just can't stop, can you? Well then, let's tackle another string...

String 4: D

Learning string 4 is like string 3 (we'll skip fret 1 again), but this time you get three notes:

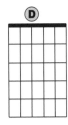
Playing string 4 open is D, written just below the staff:
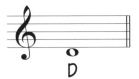

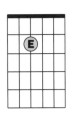
Fret 2, finger 2 is E, which occupies the first line of the staff:

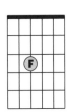
Press fret 3 with finger 3 to hear F:

21 D–E–F

Now play the new D, E, and F followed by the old D, E, and F. (We shouldn't have to tell you where they are!)

22 Same Name, Different Note

☞ Sound similar? The old D, E, and F sound one **octave** higher than the new ones. An octave means eight notes apart. You also know two more notes that are an octave apart.
HINT: string 3 open and string 1, fret 3.

Enough of that...let's jam!

Play the following exercise with your new D, E, and F (the ones on string 4, that is):

23 DEF Jam

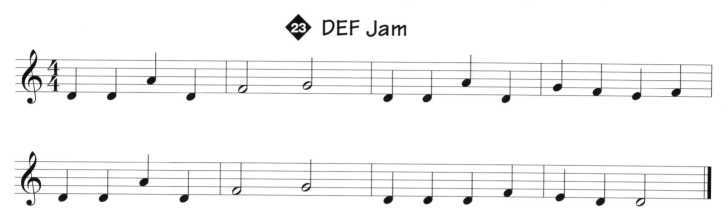

Now a tune that switches between octaves:

24 Crosswalk Blues

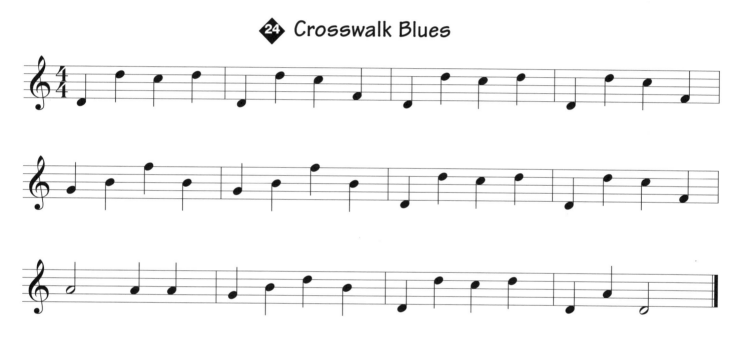

☞ FRIENDLY REMINDER: The next song is in 3/4 meter. That is, three beats (quarter notes) per measure. If you need a review, flip back to page 7.

25 House of the Rising Sun

YOU GOT RHYTHM!

Can you spare a quarter? How 'bout an eighth?

An **eighth note** has a flag on it: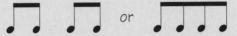

Two eighth notes equal one quarter note (or one beat in 4/4 and 3/4). To make it easier on the eyes (you're welcome), eighth notes are connected with a **beam**:

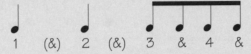

To count eighth notes, divide the beat into two and use "and" between the beats:

Practice this by first counting out loud while tapping your foot on the beat, then play the notes while counting and tapping:

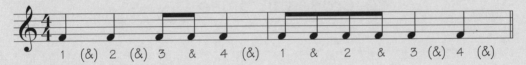

What about the rest?

Eighth rests are the same, but you...pause. Count, tap, play, and pause with the following:

Now try some songs that use eighth notes and rests. (Keep that foot going!)

26 Rockin' Riff

Excellent. But don't stop there...

20

Pickups aren't just trucks...

Instead of starting a song with rests, a **pickup measure** can be used. A pickup measure simply deletes the rests. So, if a pickup has only one beat, you count "1, 2, 3" and start playing on beat 4:

Try these songs with pickup measures:

27 Snake Charmer

28 Amazing Grace

Fantastic! Play them again and again. Remember the three Ps: practice, patience and pace yourself.

More half steps...

Let's add two more notes: another F-sharp and B-flat.

 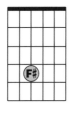

On string 4, wake up finger 4 and place it on fret 4. There's your new F-sharp.

 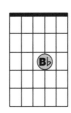

On string 3, press fret 3 with finger 3. This is B-flat, which appears on the staff like this:

29 ♦ **Minuet**

☞ Remember: A **natural** sign (♮) cancels an accidental on a note, returning it to its natural pitch.

30 ♦ **Bach Rock**

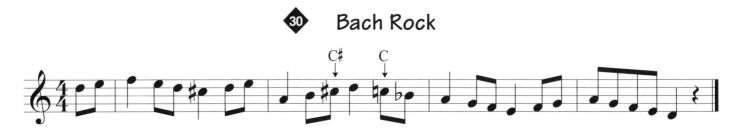

31 Alouette

☞ **Repeat signs** (𝄆 ⋯ 𝄇) tell you to (you guessed it!) repeat everything in between. If only one sign appears (𝄇), repeat from the beginning of the piece.

Here are three more great examples for your riffing pleasure (complete with repeat signs!)...

32 Hard Rock Riff

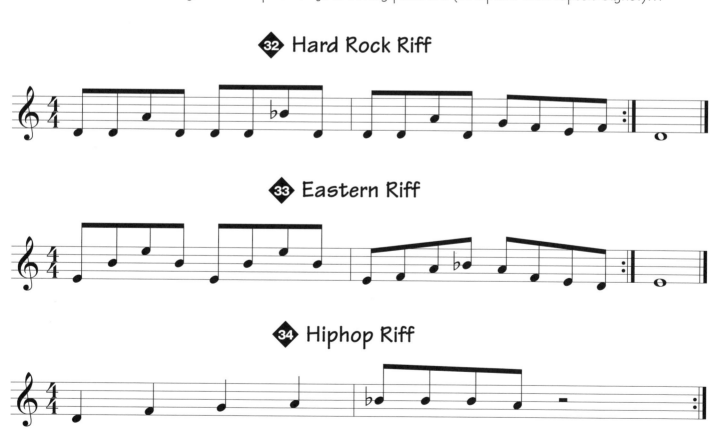

33 Eastern Riff

34 Hiphop Riff

Guitarists never die, they just go out of tune. (Make sure you're not!)

LESSON 5
Almost there...

Are you relaxed? Still in tune? Ready for another string?

String 5: A

 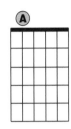

Play string 5 open. This is A. (Can you play another A? HINT: string 3.) The new A is written on two leger lines:

A

 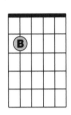

Finger and play fret 2 on string 5 and you get B. (Can you play B an octave higher?) The new B is written under just one leger line:

B

 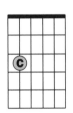

Play fret 3 of string 5 and that's C. (Where's the other C you learned?) The new C is on the first leger line:

C

Practice your new A, B, and C (slowly, of course):

35 A–B–C

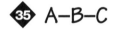

36 Run, Don't Walk

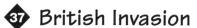

37 British Invasion

38 Drunken, Rockin' Sailor

39 Boogie Blues

WARNING: If you haven't slept since page 1, continuing could be hazardous to your enjoyment of learning the guitar. Go sleep!

YOU STILL GOT RHYTHM!

Nice tie!

A **tie** connects two notes and tells you to extend the first note to the end of the tied note:

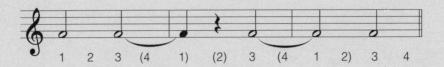

1 2 3 (4 1) (2) 3 (4 1 2) 3 4

Simple Simon! Remember to always count out loud until you begin to think and feel the beat.

The ones with dots are nice, too!

Another way to extend the value of a note is to use a **dot**. A dot extends the note by one-half of its value. Most common is the **dotted half** note:

$$\text{half note} \quad + \quad \text{dot} \quad = \quad \text{dotted half note}$$

half note   +   dot   =   dotted half note
(two beats)   (one beat)   (three beats)

You'll encounter dotted half notes in many songs, especially those that use 3/4 meter.

40 Greensleeves

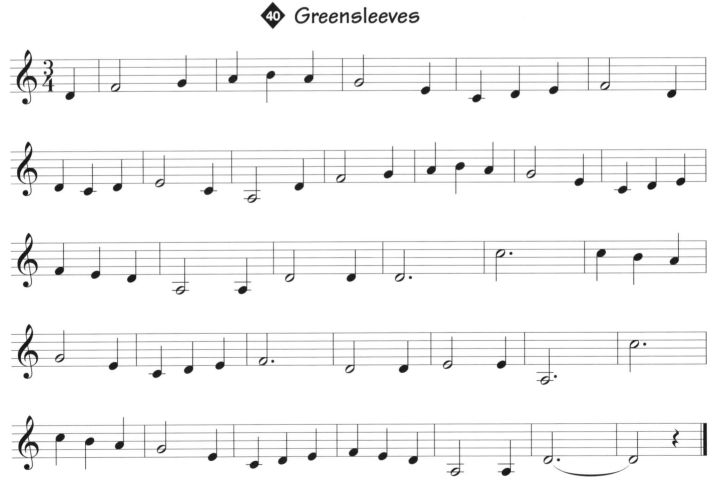

Easy as pie! Watch for the ties and dots as we continue...

26

41 Scarborough Fair

And now, please rise (but only if you have a shoulder strap)...

42 Star-Spangled Banner

LESSON 6
Last, but definitely not least...

Did you think you'd never get to the last string? Well, it's here, you're ready, let's learn it...

String 6: E

The funny thing is: you already know this string! It's exactly like string 1 (except it's thicker and sounds two octaves lower). So, every note you learned on string 1, you know the same on string 6 (a "2-for-1" special!).

 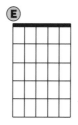 Just for kicks, play string 6 open. That's "low E." This new E (your third so far) lies just below the third leger line:

 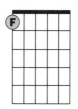 (You're already ahead of us.) Press fret 1 with finger 1 and you hear "low F."

 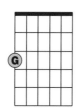 While still pressing F, press fret 3 with finger 3 and that's "low G."

43 Sixth String Strut

28

Octaves are good...

Play your new E, F, and G, followed by your first E, F, and G (on string 1, that is)...

Now add the other set of E, F, and G (on strings 4 and 3)...

☞ HELPFUL HINT: Let your eyes read ahead of the note that you're actually playing.

44 ◆ Take Me Onto the Stage, Please

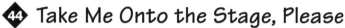

Great! But since you know all six strings, there's just no stopping. Turn the page...

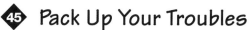

45 Pack Up Your Troubles

The next two songs have a dotted quarter note, which get one and one-half beats:

quarter note + dot = dotted quarter note
(1 beat)   (1/2 beat)   (1 1/2 beats)

Listen to the next song on the CD while you clap the beat. Can you feel the rhythm of the dotted quarter? Try playing it...

46 More Rock and Roll

Wow, those fingers can move! ("Wow, those fingers can tangle!") Practice and practice some more.

47 Battle Hymn of Rock

Oh, what the heck...here are two more notes for you (both played with finger 1)

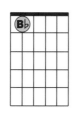

One octave lower than the previous B-flat you learned:

Bb

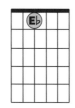

Another first fret flat (what a tongue-twister!):

Eb

48 Minor Jam

Terrific! Wanna learn to play chords? Turn the page...

LESSON 7
Fear of flying solo…

Congratulations! You know all six strings. This is a terrific time to tell you about two of guitarists' favorite things: **chords** and **tablature**.

What's a chord?

Chords consist of three or more notes played simultaneously. Listen to track 49 on the CD for some examples of chords:

49 G – Em – C – D7

Chords are good to know. For one thing, if you're feeling too lazy to play a solo melody, you can simply play the chords of a song while you sing the melody.

Introducing Tablature or "TAB"

Since chords are tricky, we'll use a special type of music notation called **tablature**. It consists of six lines (the spaces don't count), one line for each string. The number written on the line indicates which fret to play on that string:

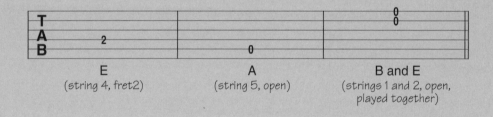

E	A	B and E
(string 4, fret2)	(string 5, open)	(strings 1 and 2, open, played together)

---

50 Tab This!

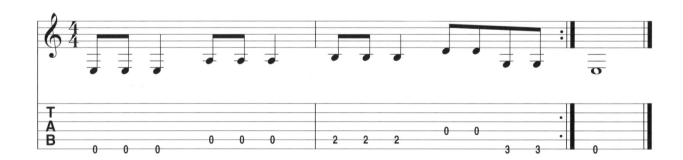

Let's dive right in and learn three commonly used **major** (we'll explain later) chords.

IMPORTANT: When playing a chord, strum only the strings that are part of the chord (the others aren't invited to the party). **Xs** above the grid tell you to avoid strumming that string; **Os** indicate an **open string**. The dots are left-hand fingerings (fingering numbers are below).

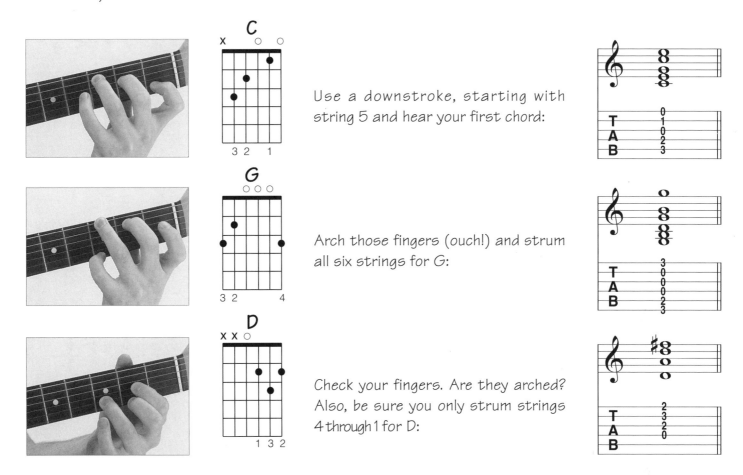

Use a downstroke, starting with string 5 and hear your first chord:

Arch those fingers (ouch!) and strum all six strings for G:

Check your fingers. Are they arched? Also, be sure you only strum strings 4 through 1 for D:

☞ A **chord line** is written above the staff (specially made for guitarists), indicating which chords to play.

51 Chord Practice

Just like single notes, a chord has rhythmic value. For example, a half-note chord gets only one strum and lasts for two beats.

In most music, chords follow certain patterns called **chord progressions**. Here is a chord progression using G–D–C:

52 Unplugged

The next song uses a common two-measure chord progression similar to many rock songs, including "Louie, Louie" and "Wild Thing."

53 Three-Chord Cliché

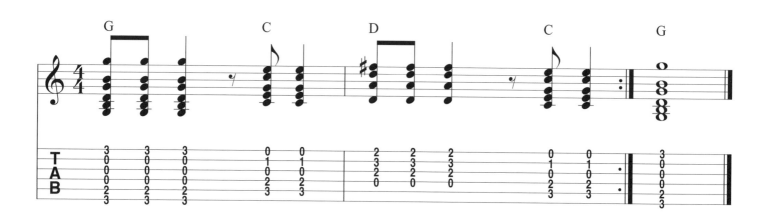

Play the following songs by reading only from the chord line. Strum once for each beat (four strums per measure). Sing along with the melody...

54 Good Night, My Fans

Good night, my fans. Good night, my fans.

Good night, my fans. I'm going to leave you now.

55 Worried Man Blues

It takes a wor - ried man to sing a wor - ried

song. It takes a wor - ried man to sing a wor - ried

song. It takes a wor - ried man to sing a wor - ried

song. I'm wor - ried now, but I won't be wor - ried long.

Now play them again and vary the number of times you strum for each chord. For example, you might want to strum along with every melody note, or just once for each chord (or maybe somewhere in the middle).

LESSON 8
It's the minor things that count...

Major chords weren't that tough, huh? How 'bout three **minor** chords?

Chords: Em, Am, and Dm

A **chord suffix** tells you what **type** of chord to play. Major chords have no suffix, only the letter name. But minor chords use the suffix "m" after the letter name.

Em

  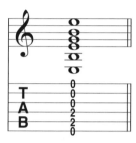

Hey, this one's easy! Smack it twice:

Am

The "low A" is the **root note** (lowest pitch) here, so be sure you avoid the sixth string when you strum:

Dm

Only the top four strings this time (just like with D major). Keep those fingers arched:

 FRIENDLY TIP: If your chord sounds bad, you probably muted or muffled a string or two. Check your fingers and play each string, one at a time, to find the "problem string(s)." Then readjust your finger(s).

Listen to these chords on the CD and then play along...take your time.

56 More Chord Practice

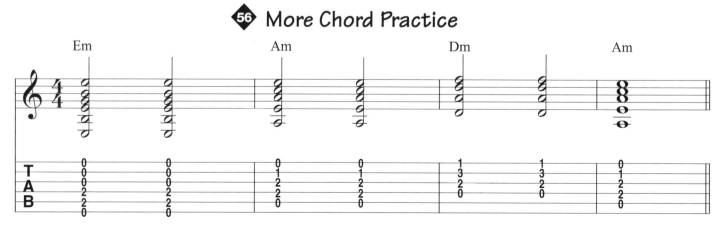

57 Chord Trax #1"

58 Chord Trax #2"

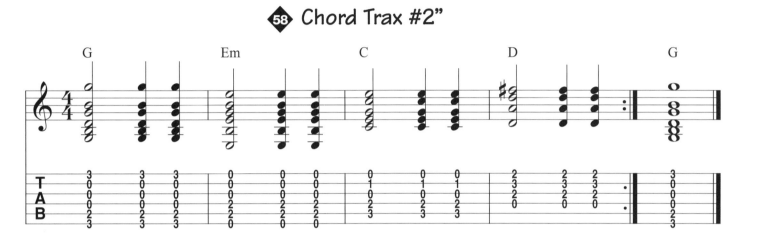

For the next example, try using an **upstrum** (↑) for the last eighth note in each measure. (That is, strum upwards starting with string 1).

59 Chord Trax #3"

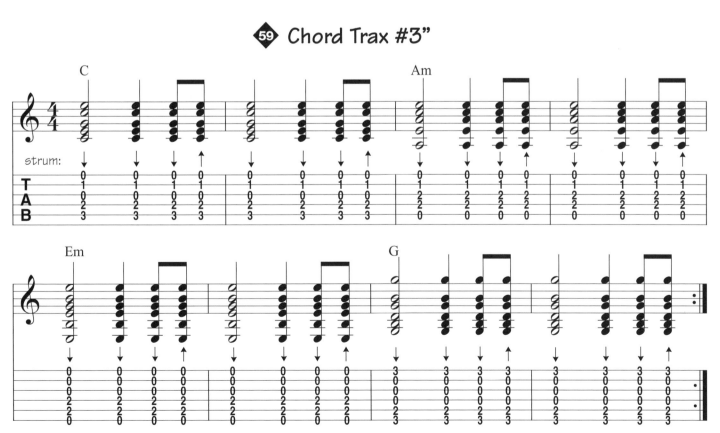

A minor question...

As you can see (and hear), a major chord is no bigger (or any more important) than a minor one, it's just a name. So what's the difference between them? Listen to them again...

QUICK AND EASY: Major chords sound "happy" and minor chords sound "sad."

Sing and use the chord line to strum along to the next two songs.

When Johnny Comes Rocking Home

61 Scarborough Fair

Are you go-ing to Scar-bor-ough Fair? Pars-ley
sage, rose-ma-ry and thyme. Re-mem-ber me to
one who lives there. ___ For once she was a true love of mine.

Sometimes, guitarists prefer to read chords from **slash notation**. (Who wouldn't? It's easier!) Strum once for every time you see a "/" symbol. The second time through, follow the chord line and try variations of downstrokes and upstrokes.

62 Chord Trax #4

63 Chord Trax #5

☞ **T**ake a break! Get something to eat, maybe some ice cream.
Then come back and really practice those chord changes again.

LESSON 9
One last note...

All six strings, major chords, minor chords—you almost know everything! Here's a new one, though...

Note: High A

Go back to string 1 (E), wake up finger 4 ("Yeah you, pinky!") and place it behind fret 5.

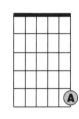

As you can see, "high A" is written on the first leger line above the staff.

A

🔮64 Just for Practice

Practice "high A" with the following two-octave exercise:

🔮65 A to A to A

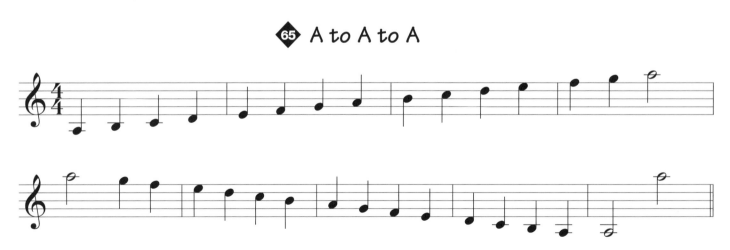

Do you realize what you just played? That was your first musical **scale**—A minor. And a two-octave scale at that!

What's a musical scale?

Scales are arrangements of notes in specific (sequential) patterns. Most scales use eight notes with the top and bottom notes being an octave apart. The one you just played started on A and used a **minor pattern**, thus it was the **A minor scale**.

Practice "high A" lots, lots more with these songs.

66 Danny Boy

Oh, Dan - ny boy, the crowd is cheer - ing for _____ you. _____ Out in their

seats, they wait for you to play. _____ And when you play, you'll

hear them sing - ing with _____ you. You are the best. At least that's what they say.

67 Auld Lang Syne

LESSON 10

You've got the power!

A great thing to know about (which a lot of beginning guitar books won't teach you) is **power chords**. These three power chords use the suffix "5."

Power Chords: E5, A5, D5

You will only play two strings at a time. **Mute** the higher ones by softly resting your right-hand palm on them.

E5

On fret 2 of strings 5 and 4, press with finger 1. Now play strings 6 and 5 only.

A5

Move finger 1 to fret 2 of string 4 and play strings 5 and 4.

D5

Move to string 3 and play strings 4 and 3.

68 Move It!

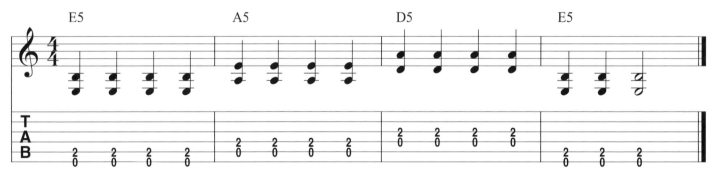

HELPFUL HINT: As you move your left hand down one string,
move your right hand down one string.

Go slowly, speed up the tempo each time you repeat, and remember to watch the music, not your fingers!

69 Power Chord Stomp

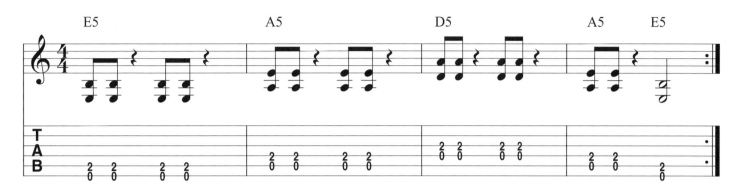

70 Movin' and Rockin'

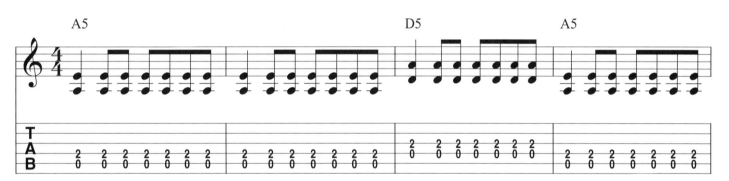

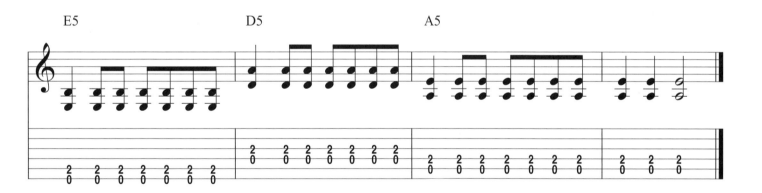

Great! Play 'em again, and by the way — *TURN IT UP!*

CAUTION: You are nearing the end of this book.
Take a break, run to your local music dealer and get **FastTrack Guitar 2!**
(You'll be glad you did.)

LESSON 11

Time to charge admission...

This isn't really a Lesson...it's a jam session!

All the FAST TRACK books (guitar, keyboard, bass and drums) have the same last section. This way, you can either play by yourself along with the CD or form a band with your friends.

So, whether the band's on the CD or in your garage, let the show begin...

71 72 Exit for Freedom

full band   minus guitar

Unplugged Ballad

75 **76** Billy B. Badd

full band   minus guitar

Bravo! Encore!!

Remember to practice often and always try to learn more about your instrument.

WAIT! DON'T GO YET!

Even though we hope (and expect) that you will review this **entire** book again and again, we thought you might like a "cheat sheet," referencing all the notes and chords you learned. Well, happy birthday!

Notes in first position:

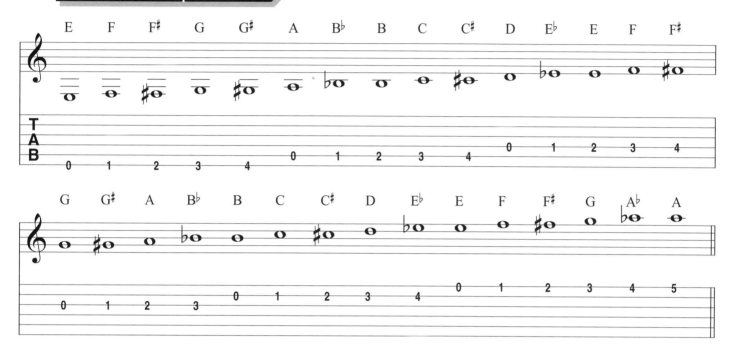

Chords in first position:

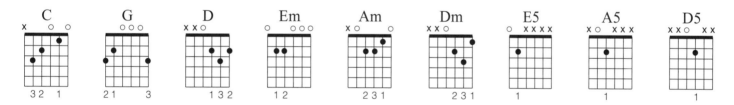

Where to go from here...

Finally, we'd like to suggest five things to help you continue to master the guitar:

1. **Repetition is the best way to learn.** Review the exercises in this book again and again until all the notes and chords are easily playable without even thinking about them.

2. **Buy "Guitar: Book 2,"** which teaches many more notes, chords, techniques, and music fundamentals. Hopefully, you can find it at the same store that had this book.

3. **Buy "Guitar: Chords and Scales,"** an excellent reference book with over 2,000 chords, as well as basic chord theory, scales, modes, and common chord progressions.

4. **Buy "Guitar: Songbook,"** which includes classic songs from The Beatles, Clapton, Hendrix, Elton John, and more!

5. **Enjoy what you do.** Whether it's practicing, picking, jamming, performing, tuning, or even cleaning your guitar, do it with a smile on your face. Life's too short.

See you next time...

SONG INDEX
(...what book would be complete without one?)